TEA IN THE NUNS' LIBRARY

Tea
In The Nuns'
Library

Jeanine Stevens

THE **BLACK SPRING**
PRESS GROUP

First published in 2022
by Eyewear Publishing Ltd.,
an imprint of Black Spring Publishing Group
United Kingdom

Typeset with graphic design by Edwin Smet
All rights reserved © 2022 Jeanine Stevens

The right of Jeanine Stevens to be identified as author of this work has been asserted in

accordance with section 77 of the Copyright, Designs and Patents Act 1988

ISBN 978-1-915406-26-2

*The editor has generally followed American spelling and punctuation
at the author's request.*

BLACKSPRINGPRESSGROUP.COM

For my grandfather Myron Harding Stevens

TABLE OF CONTENTS

AT INSIGHT COFFEE

Morning. I enjoy a mug of Rwanda blend,
a complex food item, somewhat bitter
yet holds sweetness.

I think of advice from other poets:
choose the best language,
select exquisite words,
juxtapose!

Needing another cup,
I order an Affogato, pure white gelato
with a shot of hot espresso.

A LONG WALK HOME

First freedom, beginner's rollers, felt laces
over the toe, then clamp-ons
with ball bearings, faster over cracked sidewalks.
Steel key (Chicago Skate Co.)
on a grocer's string around our necks.
We owned these streets.

Then, bikes maroon and blue, we flew past
grandfather's house, pedaling
through university grounds,
spring violets, jack-in-the-pulpits.
Out on Meridian Street to fancier homes,
up the drive, a maid flapping a kitchen towel,
shooing us like barnyard chickens.

Further out, our favorite – an abandoned estate,
matching urns with bird's nests
and cigarette butts. Crushed glass
crackling amber in the sun. Wizened pear,
crumbling steps, window's dark corridor
           – wavering profile, scant silhouette.

We sat on steps, imagined souls who lived there:
magnificent banquets, holly and red ribbons,
hired musicians and barcarolles,
uncles with sweet pipes, scent of lavender.
And in summer, white canopies,
boys with short trousers,
shrimp on toast points, imprints everywhere.
Straying too far, tires flat, a long walk home.

AFTER THE CIRCUS

Striped tents expertly folded,
equipment stored away, curlers already
wound tight in the trapeze artist's hair.

Skinny clowns wear their real faces,
walk around drinking beer,
then load tiny bikes and battered autos.

The three-legged woman climbs
aboard on two legs. Elephants
tug at chains, miss the children.

Pulling away, dark wheels grind,
screech steel-on-steel, orange sparklers
from the coal car the only light.

Next day, walk slow and you may
find a trinket in bent grass,
the scent of candy apple and hay.

SPIRIT OF THE GREEN CANOE
Camp Delight, Central Indiana

At camp, I climb down past a sign,
'Jacob's Ladder,'
to the great wooden craft at the dock.

Extra charge for lessons,
so I just imagine the river's quiet glide.
Sun perch nibble air,
summer grasses flower and curl
on sleepy banks.
I come to a soft bend, paddle up,
rest in a small cove, realize I cannot swim.

I feel the memory of Tecumseh,
trading his fallen timbers,
thirty million acres for a small split of land,
no deer, no bear, negotiations
at a standstill. I marvel
at the Shawnee mind trying to unify tribes
who speak twenty languages.
Yet none of this taught in school,
only 'Tippecanoe and Tyler Too!'

Did he stop here letting his horse drink long?
He knew betrayal at his heels,
heels that knew flanks so well, heels
that drove him on.

He could be here in summer's dust
rethinking the idea of coalition,

watchful, patient with time.
As he said:
'We have no place else to go.'

Late afternoon; steady hands
ease me back to shore.

IN THIS ROOM EVERYONE BEHAVED

I'm at the front door, remembering
the light panel, the pane that cut my hand.
A boy struck my sister with a piece of coal;
I was frantically knocking for help.
Inside the living room, I'm looking at the baby grand
where mother and grandfather played tunes by ear:
'Little Brown Jug,' and 'The Hawaiian Love Call.'
I see the bench filled with advanced sheet music,
Czerny and Bach, and my own beginner's
John Thompson with a few faded stars and flags
on barely learned pieces, and in front of the fireplace,
andirons with carved bear profiles. In the corner
sat the Philco with its green eye.
Look, I'm there with my brother on Saturday morning
listening to 'Let's Pretend,' or writing down
instructions for the number of box tops
needed for a Wonder Woman ring.
Here is the stack of *Life* Magazines
that came every Friday and reported every war.
This room was a place where we all behaved,
where the insurance man sat on the sofa to renew policies.
Near the front window, the Christmas tree glittered
in a swath of angel hair and Noma lights.
This is where we acted up when the sitter
(old Mrs. Selby) came; we did cartwheels,
tossed popcorn and were sent to bed.
The night my Dad worked swing shift,
a young sitter had a party, the room filled with sailors.
Next morning Schlitz beer cans dotted the lawn
and neighbors clucked their tongues.

The drapes with cabbage roses are missing,
the designer wallpaper gone.
A family fist fight required a call to the cops.
I recall the aroma of pork chops, the soft clink of china
as mother hand-washed the dishes.
See us in front of the radio for the news
or a comedy? Dad rests in his chair, smokes
a Lucky Strike and reads *The Indianapolis Star*.
In this room – we all behaved.

SEVENTY-FIVE MILES FROM THE BORDER

A vacant stretch – Route #66, 11 pm... the family rests
alongside the road. The gray hulking house trailer, bought
secondhand with cash from grandfather's farm, sits exhausted
against the shoulder. Inside, the air reeks: overripe cantaloupe,
canned spaghetti, baby diapers and Pall Mall cigarettes.

The girl and boy pull their wooly Hudson Bay blankets onto
the sand between barrel-shaped sagebrush. They know nothing
about scorpions and prickly cactus, only leeches, chiggers
and water moccasins. She places new sandals, woven straw,
white elastic straps, side by side next to the blanket. Purchased
yesterday in Gallup, the girl wonders if they will be in style.

Navy and orange stripes scratch, but she drifts off into faint
pink light toward the west. The boy – not minding scratchy
things, settles in, faces oncoming big rigs, the bright glare
stirring dreams. He will get a job and restore Classic Chevys.
Tomorrow, they will be Californians.

PALETTE

Green-blue. Some cultures have one word,
splashing all the lovely shades together.
How then to differentiate
between seafoam and ocular fuzz, cadet
and midnight, cerulean and cobalt?

Perhaps people of earth
who focus more on animal tracks,
the need to separate the elephant's dark depth,
the giraffe's ochre skin, to separate
the spear's carmine blood
from evening's rose-gold flame,
scarlet from the seep of tribal scar,
the russet prick of ash mixed with flesh.

How to distinguish between the four hues
of this vast alpine lake
where forest blends with sky,
blends with summer at the edge of violet.
In a new box of crayons, I wanted:
yellow-green, violet-red, blue-black,
the entire spectrum.

Green, so vegetative, how much you need
your own hues: brilliant horn worm,
thick chartreuse pollen.
In the hedgerows, blue is miniscule
as in berries and shadow.
But the blend: aquamarine, turquoise,
essential to explain the peacock's fan, Navaho
squash blossom, the morning glory pool.

TONY'S ON THE PIER

Redondo Beach, California

Here with cousins in the 1950's,
met my first love on the sand,
wild in the scent of burnt skin, salt and sweat.

The splintered observation deck overlooks
a weary Pacific. I talk to others here
on recommendations from Trip Advisor.

Mine is not a casual visit but one to say goodbye,
a last relative from all those
who came west to work in the industry:
Hughes, Boeing, Douglas.

The Foster Freeze is gone,
and the thrift shop where we bought
out-of-date Navy uniforms,
a white sharkskin blazer with gold buttons
I wore all through high school.

On the bar, a souvenir, larger than a shot glass,
probably an Old Fashioned style,
touristy design. Sturdy pilasters
support the deck, inky waves reach underneath,
black palms clump near a vacant shore
and somewhere the soundtrack, *Victory at Sea.*

BLACK ICE & POETRY

Shops that cater to vacationers closed.
If you want a post card or souvenir shot glass,
check out the local CVS.
The slow cadence of late Autumn, a good time
to check the spatter of moth holes
on wool cardigans.
Snow limits choices.

A local bookseller remains open.
Hardy poets stage a costume party:
one dressed as Sexton curses a dog,
another as Hefner in a silk dressing gown
looks amused. Someone brings absinthe.
Black ice appears on the road.

A pause before the Italians arrive,
blond women and dark haired men,
designer ski togs and gold jewelry,
antsy to hit the slopes.
Locals pack a lunch, retreat to the lake
and count the bald eagles nesting.

WINTER COAT TINGED PLATINUM
South Lake Tahoe

To the city yard for sand bags to plug
the hole where the raccoon dug under the cabin.
Between flurries, a walk in the pines.

Ahead, 100 yards: a coyote crosses the road,
fluffy white, yellow, gray like a big blond fox.
I stop, raise my arm in salute
not sure if this is a right gesture.

            Watching, turning
                toward me, a long time.

(Something familiar, head and shoulders foreshortened
like the giraffe pictograph in the Fezzan,
North Africa, 100 B.C.
            Same stance, hesitation,
no threat, something beyond,   curiosity?)

I look back to see if I'm being followed.
No.
He trots on, probably to trash bins
behind Safeway,
winter coat tinged platinum,
curved back mimics
Mount Rose in the distance.

Later, sitting by the woodstove snapping cedar,
what to make of contact with topaz eyes,
             wild fur, the edge of things?

I think artifact,
look at my Washoe basket, buck saw,
map of prehistoric game trails.

The cabin warms; ice chunks slide
from the tin roof.
On the Tamarack, a Red-headed Woodpecker
chisels out another unwritten code.

TEA IN THE NUNS' LIBRARY

Returning to San Francisco from the UK,
lengthy customs check, I miss my connecting bus
to the valley, the next at 7 am.
In the hollow terminal, weary passengers
wait for unscheduled planes,
the only sound, soft clink of baggage carts.

Scent pillows bulging with dried freesias leak
through my canvas bag – so far from the gift shop
at Avebury. There are no fences at Stonehenge;
touch the Heel Stone if you want!

My body makes a lumpy sculpture,
slumping on the hard bench, purse strapped
on like a parachute, valuables tucked inside my shirt,
the pinkish Queen sweating with the odor of old money.
I phone my ex-boyfriend.
He changed his number.

All through the night a transient sits across from me.
I could say political things are happening
like Nixon resigning, but that was seven years ago.
'Sleep my child and peace attend thee.'

Near Oxford, skinheads are turned away,
instead firebomb a small pub near Epwell Rectory.

My bus ride to Sacramento will hold sadness:
no swans, no choirboys singing
at St. Martins in the Fields,

only the Jelly Belly Factory, Budweiser Tasting Room
and the dry hills of American Canyon.

Does San Francisco still exist? All is darkness except
corridors of light on runways made of ground-down
shellfish, flattened mounds of the Ohlone people.

At a newsstand, I glance at the British issue
of *Time Magazine*. Skinheads made full cover,
yet stateside, only a small spark in the inset.

I could mention the performance
of *A Midsummer Night's Dream* at Stratford,
fairies as clacking wood puppets,
battery-operated lights in their hair,
and in *A Winter's Tale*, all costumes spun white.

I could mention my slow boat ride to Abingdon
on Sunday (see the postcard), tea in the Nuns' library,
relaxing in the fragrant blend of oranges and scones.

I slip into my tutor's room (an expert
in English Landscapes). A heavy build, says he
is Welsh. Notes from *Porgy and Bess*
drift up from the student dorms.

At his lodge on my last day,
a garden lunch among roses: bright table linens,
china, salads, cold-spiced fish prepared by a wife
who looks serious. And plenty of wine.

TIDAL ISLAND, NORTHUMBERLAND

By the priory, a fat pigeon pecks along the greening walk.
Burgundy tulips bloom large in russet pots
and wicker frames support wild roses against rock walls.
A side path leads to the sea and a lesser island,
only 1/4 acre, separated by high tide.
Eider ducks squabble.
Winter thistle scrapes my calf.

Near the cliff, someone tied a thick rope to a tree.
I lower myself down. Fossil remains
of a sea crinoid lie strewn at the shoreline,
star-shaped calyx and broken stems said to resemble
a saint's beads. Murky water,
a steel-tipped sky seems fitting
for solitude. I wade out.
Is that low mound a beehive-shaped cell,
a recluse retreat? I hesitate.

In a time before I wore shoes, I sat
in silence on the banks of a canal, drowsy in the rhythm
of each ripple, so measured,
so different from the last.
Not paying attention, I slipped under
a motorboat's wake, tangled roots on muddy walls
in silty water impossible to grab.
Grandfather in his Sunday suit jumped in,
pulled me out by my hair. He gave me
my first Bible, my first gold locket.

Then older, leaving for my date, I still
see him at the door, 'Could you please pick up
my chewing tobacco while you're out?'
a crumpled bill in his hand. I waved him off –
too busy. I did cook his meals, drive him
to appointments, flew his gray coffin
with chrome latches back to Indiana.
How many rights does it take to fix a wrong?

Turning back to the mainland, I watch wind
tousle sea pinks, then remember his favorite song,

'The Bells of St. Mary's, the loved ones,
the dear ones who come from the sea.'

I'm certain I hear seals singing
even now.

HILLY FLANKS

We learned about the delicate valley sketched
in turquoise on our pull-down school map.

The Tigris-Euphrates seemed
a dreamy Eden, sparking gem, squint

of glass flowers, like Swarovski crystals:
orange speckled lily, ruby striped dahlia.

A lush promise –
now rude vines, scarred and stripped.

Crumpled blooms at the edge of burned citadels
fall; charred seeds dig deep.

As she writes a letter home, a few kernels
fall into her uniform's soiled cuff

perhaps to find wet banks, slumber
then germinate in a future greening time.

PURPLE MOUNTAINS MAJESTY

After a photo by David Woodfall

Tucked together,
sedans and rusty panel trucks
slump, doors gape, fenders
sprout stiff prairie grass,
sagging tires the first to rot.

Newer models sit high on the horizon,
lift bright hoods: slick red, yellow
and aqua enamel sparkling in the sunlight.
Perhaps they will be rescued for parts?

But tonight, no one walks here.
It seems a vast sacrifice at the base
of these ancient Rockies made purple
only by their distance.
Discarded, they silently decompose,
moonlight leveling shape and shadow.

SAND

After Carl Sandburg's 'Grass.'

I am not grass, doing the work at Agincourt,
Flanders Fields, Gettysburg. I say

bulldoze them under, layer bodies in strata
mottled khaki fabric, trenches eons deep.

A nomad's unmarked grave: Chaldea,
Kirkuk, Haladja, Tobruk. Strands, threads

and tallow. Barely audible voices
tumble from hanging towers, dimmest
shapes, then, wise men leaving on horseback.

In five years or ten, other caravans will ask,
'Was this a city, a village, a tribe?'

Maybe in 4,000 years, storms will come again,
travelers scattering glass between two rivers.

I am sand; I obliterate borders; let me work.

EDGING EXOTIC INTO CONSCIOUSNESS

White space as breath holds narrow interstice, a small pocket
that grows multitudinous inhaling the entire Arctic Sea.
                The scent of balsam

as from stately firs is gobbled up as fragrance by hungry
lungs. Incense becomes smoke, slips down vessel and tissue
                to mid-section. Even if

tarnished like an acid-etched mirror, belly wants its share,
devours all, nothing frittered away. Rumblings of metaphor,
                the is ness

of mulled-over images chewed into morsels, reformed,
released to rest in golden channels. The conduit is assembled,
                the smoke extinguished.

If my thigh feels chafed and I rubbed hard enough,
what would emerge? This great human shank sprung from
                the center of green?

TERZANELLE IN ARLES

At the night café lamps burn for hours,
buildings glowing in sepia tones.
I walk narrow streets searching for flowers,

measure my steps over slick cobblestones.
Here comes the postman holding good news,
buildings glowing in sepia tones.

See how sturdy his dusty black shoes.
I vandalized billboards; how can I lose?
Here comes the postman holding good news.

Graffiti and scraps stimulate my muse,
while the mistral blasts down from the canyon.
I vandalized billboards: how can I lose?

Pigeons grasp tight to rungs near the fountain.
In the distance – a yellow house and blue chair,
while the mistral blasts down from the canyon.

Note the small mirror for trimming one's hair;
in the distance – a yellow house and blue chair.
At the night café lamps burn for hours,
I walk narrow streets searching for flowers.

FACULTY OFF-SITE: FOLSOM PRISON

At the stone gate, it takes forever to clear security: rings,
watch, keys, buckles; one of us needs
multiple passes to disentangle a complicated
hairdo, hairpins triggering alarms.

I think of the old trick: key-hole saw
hidden in a birthday cake.

Walking through the open yard
into a smudge of denim, so many who won't
receive training, a week's severance pay.

(We later learn this was a misdirect –
no outsiders allowed in the Yard).

Steel cuts air – we sit in a classroom,
witness an experiment in recidivism:
brief coffee, short testimonials.

Officials arrive, escort us outside granite walls
to the visitor's dining hall.
Lunch is steak with serrated knife,
potatoes, green beans with bacon
and nubby sweet Gherkins.

One of our colleagues, raised in an embattled country,
is unable to eat, or speak.
Silence seems the right thing to do.
No one wants apple pie.

Noon sun steams black.
Guards in towers resemble dark squares,
lean like cardboard cut-outs.

I will remember well the blaze of denim.

We were told not to wear blue.

CAMPUS NOCTURNE

In order to keep my retirement, I'm summoned
back to campus (without pay, no parking pass;
the fees will eat up my sensible shoes).
I have no supplies, gave tapes and CDs away,
thirty years of texts and resource books.

Now the halls narrow, cloistered incense
and dust, faceless gargoyles at their dusk.
No mailbox, no office space. I'm ordered not
to attend faculty meetings (a good thing).
A locust brings a note written on a corn husk:
'The syllabus must deal with Ethnography,
 and include the words: *reciprocity, purity and danger.*'

My students are wild turkeys grazing
on the edge of the football field, tough old birds
in sneakers sitting askew, blue webbed feet
dangling, craws bulging with ideas.

Holding class in a feed store, I assign the final essay:
'Support the idea that all first words were one syllable,'
(grit, stone, cluck). Since turkeys have no hands
they cannot fill bluebooks; I make this an oral exam;
they all gabble oblique concepts – credit/no credit.

I go to the Health Center for a B.P. check –
they say I have no pulse.

DOLL OF LOVED PARTS

I rummage in my box of discards
purchased from an estate sale: split arms,
fractured legs, overlarge stuffed bodies.
Various heads don't match.

I could assemble a person of parts
who was loved so much:
grabbed by the hair, swung around
until an arm came loose –
better than being ignored.

I remember the autistic boy
for years stroking
a stuffed duck he named Gary.
When new, bright yellow,
but over time, so much cradling,
Gary lost his fuzz.
Eventually rubbed down
to a miniature pelt
shiny as satin, the scrap
is still tacked to the man's CD cabinet.

Laying out my finds, I discover
I have enough to do multiples,
an entire diorama of loved parts.

PAINTED ANIMALS

Removing lawns, woody roses,
making way for stream beds
and native perennials, a small plastic gladiator
pokes out of the dry bank: white toga,
gold helmet and breastplate. Someone's toy
or one of Caesar's lost legions?

Did Roman children have carved soldiers
with swords to dismember starving beasts?

Son and daughter always requested 'animal sets'
for birthdays: tigers and lions,
cowboys and buffalos,
even prehistoric Rex and pterodactyls.

When new, kept inside until paint wore off,
then scattered around two acres, riding in Tonka Trucks,
lined up on railings by the stables,
some even strapped to balsa wood airplanes.
Where did they all get to?

Fascinating, the remnants of play days.
As a child, restaurants with little tables
and handmade menus the most fun.
When we moved,
Aunt Frances found a green glass
toy cup and saucer on the back step.

I try to remember 'child mind,'
an entire afternoon filled
with Amazonian jungles, gilded lunch rooms,
vast prairies, grand coliseums.

WINTER HOLIDAY

We come to deal with grief and avoid solitude:
walking Union Square, coffee shops
and well-dressed people, then the lobbies
of grand hotels with ornate staircases.

Watching the lighting of the tree
from the Starlight Lounge twenty-one floors up,
we pay a fortune for high-end drinks.

We do not have roast turkey with oyster stuffing,
no pecan pie, no freshly ironed linen cloth,
no centerpiece of winter squash.

Instead, Pacific salmon, wild rice and tiramisu
at a small table with other tourists, some
complaining the salmon is undercooked.

Next day, past bustling Chinatown
we visit North Beach, tables set al fresco:
Today's Special: Rigatoni and Chianti.

We backtrack to City Lights Books, finally
relax in the overstuffed chairs in the poetry section.
I purchase *Saving Twilight*, Julio Cortázar,
caught by his photo sitting on the floor,
smiling, so happy talking to his cat.

Heading home, on our left, Alcatraz,
the lone stone edifice
– Corso's deserted holiday.

When we enter the family room,
the unopened box of decorations:
angels and snowflakes made by tiny hands.

NOTES

'Winter Coat Tinged Platinum' was inspired by Tony Kendrew's poem, 'Coyote', *Feathers Scattered in the Wind*, The Welsh Writing Desk, 2014.

'Sand' is after Carl Sandburg's poem, 'Grass', *Cornhuskers*, 1918.

'Terzanelle in Arles', the images come from paintings by Vincent Van Gogh.

Saving Twilight, Julio Cortázar, Pocket Poets Number 53, City Lights Books, San Francisco, 1997.

ACKNOWLEDGEMENTS

Grateful acknowledgements to the editors of the following journals in which these poems first appeared.

'After the Circus,' *California Quarterly*; 'Campus Nocturne,' *Chiron Review*; 'Palette,' *Colere*; 'Hilly Flanks,' *Written Here, Community of Writers*; 'Black Ice and Poetry,' *Convergence*; 'Seventy-Five Miles from the Border,' *Desert Voices*; 'Edging Exotic into Consciousness,' *Edge*; 'Tidal Island, Northumberland,' 'Spirit of the Green Canoe,' *Exit 13*; 'Winter Coat Tinged Platinum,' 'Faculty Off-Site at Folsom Prison,' *Forge*; 'Sand,' *Poetry Depth Quarterly*; 'In This Room Everyone Behaved,' *Provincetown Magazine*; 'Tony's on the Pier,' *Sacramento Voices 2018*; 'A Long Walk Home,' *So It Goes – Journal of the Kurt Vonnegut Memorial Library*; 'Terzanelle in Arles,' *The MacGuffin*; 'Doll of Loved Parts,' *Tipton Poetry Review*; 'Purple Mountains Majesty,' *Westwind Review*.

'In This Room Everyone Behaved,' won the WOMR Cape Cod Community Radio National Award.

Gratitude to Josh McKinney, Kim Addonizio, Alexa Mergen, and Linda Pickens-Jones, who advised on early drafts of some poems. And as always, Greg Chalpin.

A special thank you to Eyewear Publishing and especially Dr. Todd Swift for his encouragement and support, Amira Ghanim for her enthusiasm and diligence and Cate Myddleton-Evans for her sensibility to the poems and her excellent editing. Thanks also to Edwin Smet for his skillful typesetting.

Death *in the* Grizzly Maze